THE BRITISH MUSEUM

LEONARDO
DA VINCI
AND HIS CIRCLE

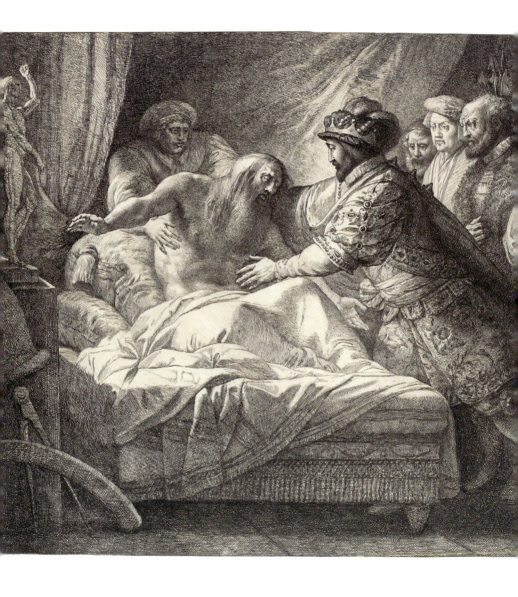

THE BRITISH MUSEUM

LEONARDO DA VINCI
AND HIS CIRCLE

Claire Van Cleave

THE BRITISH MUSEUM PRESS

© 2008 The Trustees of the British Museum

Claire Van Cleave has asserted the right to be identified as the author of this work

First published in 2008 by The British Museum Press
A division of The British Museum Company Ltd
38 Russell Square, London WC1B 3QQ
www.britishmuseum.org

A catalogue record for this book is available from the British Library

ISBN 978-0-7141-2662-3

Frontispiece: Giuseppe Cades,
Leonardo da Vinci on his deathbed embraced by King Francis 1st of France,
late 1770s, print, 455 x 555 mm (detail)

Photography by the British Museum Department of Photography and Imaging
Designed and typeset in Centaur by Peter Ward
Printed in China by C&C Offset Printing Co., Ltd

Leonardo da Vinci

(1452–1519)

THE LEGEND OF LEONARDO taking his last breath in the arms of his patron the king of France comes from Giorgio Vasari's account (1568) of the life of the great Florentine artist. The etching by Giuseppe Cades (1750–99) depicting Leonardo's deathbed (frontispiece) attests to the enduring and still inextinguishable fame of Leonardo. His genius is exceptional even by twenty-first-century standards. Few if any polymaths in history have equalled Leonardo's diverse talents in the fields of art, architecture, science, maths and engineering. What is extraordinary is that Leonardo's knowledge of these fields was not superficial, but profound in each subject.

Leonardo was primarily an artist, and yet, despite the perennial fame of the *Mona Lisa* and the *Last Supper*, it is surprising that his career as a painter cannot be easily measured by his output. In fact, the dating of Leonardo's works is notoriously difficult because he laboured over projects for decades and then frequently left them unfinished. His unusually curious mind, which led him to design ambitious compositions and to use experimental techniques, was more interested in creation than in execution, with the result that important works such as the Sforza equestrian monument or the mural depicting the *Battle of Anghiari* either were never completed or disintegrated. The best way to assess Leonardo's career is to plot his travels from his youth in Florence through his death in France.

As a young man, Leonardo was a member of the workshop of the great Florentine sculptor, goldsmith and painter Andrea del Verrocchio

(1435–88). Verrocchio also seems to have loved designing sculptures and paintings, but he employed a team of capable assistants to bring his ideas to fruition. Verrocchio's own spectacular drawings show the fundamental importance of drawing in his workshop and Leonardo's own earliest sketches show Verrocchio's influence, but, unlike his master, Leonardo drew with his left hand, so his drawings are easily distinguishable.

Under Verrocchio's tutelage, Leonardo worked closely alongside the painters Lorenzo di Credi (1459–1537) and Pietro Perugino (*c*.1450–1523). Undoubtedly Leonardo would also have learned about sculpture, as masterpieces in stone, terracotta and metal were also an important part of Verrocchio's output, but his primary work was completing paintings to Verrocchio's designs. Vasari tells the story that Leonardo painted the kneeling angels on the lower left of Verrocchio's *Baptism of Christ* (Uffizi, Florence) with such talent that from then on Verrocchio put down his own brush and colours in deference to the great talent of his pupil.

In the late 1470s Leonardo started to paint independently of his master. By 1478, he had completed the portrait of *Ginevra de' Benci* (National Gallery of Art, Washington, DC), initiated two representations of the Virgin and been awarded his first important commission, for an altarpiece for the chapel of San Bernardo in the Palazzo della Signoria. The latter was never finished, foreshadowing the fate of many of Leonardo's works. In 1481 Leonardo was given the job of painting an altarpiece for the main altar of San Donato a Scopeto. The picture he designed for the convent never came to fruition, despite a rigid time schedule set out in the commissioning documents. An unfinished monochrome painting of the *Adoration of the Magi* (Uffizi, Florence) is assumed to be the work Leonardo abandoned when he left Florence for Milan around 1482, because it matches the San Donato commission in size and subject. A number of extant preliminary drawings (opposite and pp. 40–45)

Detail of Leonardo's left-handed hatching, in
A man blowing a trumpet into the ear of a nude man (see p. 43),
c.1480–81, pen and ink over stylus.

demonstrate Leonardo's ambitious plans for this altarpiece, but it is unclear whether he cast the work aside because he lost interest in the painting or because he had set his sights on becoming a court artist in Milan.

Leonardo arrived in Milan sometime between September 1481 and April 1483 and presented himself to Ludovico Sforza as a multi-talented artist, architect and engineer who, among many other things, could make the long-standing idea for a gigantic equestrian monument of Francesco, the first Sforza duke, a reality. This project engaged Leonardo's thoughts for most of the next twenty years. During this first Milanese period, Leonardo initiated the *Virgin of the Rocks* (Louvre, Paris), another project that took years to be realized. Other paintings thought to date from this time include the *Lady with an ermine* (Museum Czartoryskich, Krakow) and further representations of the Virgin and Child. Simultaneously, he became involved with designs for the domed crossing of Milan Cathedral, a project that occupied him from 1487 to 1490, when the job was given to a rival architect. If this were not enough, Leonardo was also designing ephemeral decorations for the marriage of Gian Galeazzo Sforza, duke of Milan, and later for the marriage of his uncle Ludovico.

During the last decade of the fifteenth century, Leonardo was the foremost artist in Milan and effectively in the employ of the Sforza duke and his family. Records show that he was running a busy workshop of artists including the painters Marco d'Oggiono and Giovanni Antonio Boltraffio (pp. 78–9). This is also the period when Leonardo began to jot down his theories on art in various notebooks. Work on the monumental sculpture of Francesco Sforza on horseback progressed from drawings to a clay model, but although bronze was set aside for its manufacture, it was not cast. In 1494, Leonardo's long-standing patron Ludovico Sforza finally assumed the ducal throne after the assassination of his nephew. Around this time Leonardo was commissioned to paint the *Last Supper* surmounted by the Sforza arms in the refectory of Santa Maria delle Grazie. Notwithstanding Leonardo's experimental technique and the rapid deterioration of the mural, this painting has become one of the iconic images of Western art. Also around this time he took up red chalk as a drawing tool (see pp. 61 and 65), creating exceptional drawings in both red and black chalk (Royal Collection, Windsor Castle) as studies for the Apostles in the mural.

By 1498 the Sforza horse was still not realized in bronze, but descriptions relate that the sculpture was intended to be over ten metres high and would require 150,000 pounds of bronze for completion. In the same year, the crowning of Louis XII as king of France changed the fortunes of Milanese politics and thus the career of Leonardo. Whereas Ludovico Sforza had courted the previous French king and had assuaged French aggression into Italian territory, Louis XII was not so easily appeased and stormed Milan in the early days of September 1499. Ludovico was captured and sent to France, and the model for the Sforza horse on which Leonardo had laboured for over sixteen years was destroyed. Leonardo survived, but the political turmoil forced him to leave Milan.

In the first few years of the sixteenth century, Leonardo established relationships with members of the French court and travelled from Milan to Rome where Cesare Borgia, son of Pope Alexander VI, employed him as their 'family architect and general engineer'. By 1503 Leonardo had returned to Florence. In order to stir up interest in his arrival and show off his talent, Leonardo exhibited a large, highly finished cartoon of the *Virgin and Child with SS. Anne and John the Baptist* (National Gallery, London, p. 12) which, according to Vasari, crowds flocked to see during its two-day public display. Florence had also undergone political change with the expulsion of the Medici and their replacement in 1494 with a new Republican government. Piero Soderini, head of the government, seized upon the unusual opportunity of having the two foremost living Florentine artists resident in the city and commissioned Leonardo and Michelangelo to paint murals in the council chamber of the Palazzo della Signoria (see pp. 53, 55 and 69). The fame of Leonardo's designs and the public display of his large cartoon for the central scene depicting the *Fight for the Standard* ensured that even though the mural rapidly decayed because of his disastrous experimental technique, images of it have survived through copies and written accounts. In addition to the *Battle of Anghiari* mural, Leonardo was engaged with various engineering works for Florence and its allies. Other painting projects datable to this second Florentine period include the now-lost *Salvator Mundi* and the beginning of work on the lost or never-painted *Leda and the Swan* (see pp. 86–9) and the *Portrait of Mona Lisa*, which remained with Leonardo until his death in France.

In late 1506 Leonardo left Florence and returned to Milan where he was employed by Charles d'Amboise, the French governor of Milan. The Florentine government imposed strict rules on Leonardo to protect the agreement to complete the Anghiari mural, but negotiations with the French court in Milan eventually released Leonardo from his promises. A disappointed Soderini wrote, 'He has taken a good portion of the money and has made a small beginning of a large work he was supposed to do'. The following years were filled with legal disputes over the Anghiari mural and the still unfinished *Virgin of the Rocks*. Nevertheless, Leonardo remained in Milan to serve the occupying French government. He was briefly in Florence in 1508 but until 1513 resided mainly in Milan. Around 1508 he began a painting of the *Virgin and Child with St Anne* (Louvre, Paris), which was based on the large cartoon exhibited in Florence a few years earlier (p. 12). Other works of this date include forays into anatomical and mathematical problems and the design of waterworks and other engineering jobs, which were recorded in drawings and notes written in his own unique left-handed backwards script in notebooks such as the so-called Codex Leicester (collection of Bill and Melinda Gates, Seattle, Washington), which is filled with dense scribbles and marginal drawings.

By 1513 Leonardo's career had taken another turn because of the political fortunes of his patrons. In 1511 French control of Milan ended, and in the next year Soderini's Republican government fell and the Medici family returned to power in Florence. Their consolidation of power culminated in the election of Giovanni de'Medici as Pope Leo X in 1513. The sixty-one-year-old Leonardo allied himself with the pope's brother Giuliano and moved into apartments in the Belvedere in the Vatican palace. In the two years that Leonardo resided in Rome, Michelangelo had recently completed the Sistine ceiling and Raphael was hard at work on the frescoes in the Vatican *stanze*. It is interesting to imagine what the aged Leonardo might have thought of these important painting commissions. Surely he would have marvelled at the artists' abilities to complete such large-scale projects. Leonardo's own work of this period was confined to maps and engineering projects to drain marshes for the pope and continuing work on unfinished pictures for other patrons.

Upon the death of Giuliano de'Medici in 1516 Leonardo wrote, 'The Medici made me and destroyed me', and yet, as so many times before, Leonardo's career benefited from a regime change. Later that year he moved to France at the invitation of the French king Francis I, and there he lived out his remaining years in a substantial house at Cloux, part of the royal estate at Amboise. He took with him his faithful servant Giacomo Salaì and his devoted pupil and companion

Francesco Melzi, and together all three men received stipends from the king. Leonardo occupied himself with various architectural and engineering projects and continued to collate his manuscripts into treatises, but it appears that the king paid Leonardo a pension just to have the great genius under his roof. There is no contemporary account of Leonardo actually dying in the arms of the king (see frontispiece), but when he did expire on 2 May 1519, Francis undoubtedly mourned for his immensely gifted courtier.

The painter Francesco Melzi, whom Leonardo had first met in 1507, was the executor of Leonardo's estate and inherited his remaining drawings, manuscripts and artistic tools. Melzi continued to organize Leonardo's writings into publishable form, eventually completing a treatise on painting. Because of the numerous unfinished projects and the transitory nature of the *Battle of Anghiari* and the *Last Supper*, Leonardo's preserved manuscripts and surviving drawings form an important part of our knowledge of the artist. The British Museum is fortunate to have over twenty-one original sheets by Leonardo, many with drawings on both sides of the page. The Museum's holdings illustrated in the pages of this book are strongest in figural drawings from the first part of Leonardo's long career but also contain examples from works of later years. They are here supplemented by sheets in the Museum's collection attributed to Leonardo's close followers, which demonstrate the artistic legacy of his great genius.

The Virgin and Child with SS. Anne and John the Baptist,
*c.*1500, charcoal and black and white chalks, 141.5 x 106 cm.

As a student in Verrocchio's workshop, Leonardo would have been familiar with the practice of making drapery studies with a brush on linen to understand the volume and lighting of a figure clothed in heavy garments. The models for these studies were often mannequins draped in cloth dipped in liquid plaster that hardened to form a long-lasting pattern which could be patiently studied over a length of time without change to the arrangement of the folds. In this example, Leonardo barely sketched in the outline of the figure whereas he laboured in detail over the highlights and shadows of the brightly lit mantle. The sculptural quality of the folds is heightened by the contrast of the dark background with the white highlighting used to create the greatest part of the drapery. Effective rendering of folds of heavy fabric enabled the Renaissance artist to impart volume and animation to stationary figures.

Study of drapery for a kneeling woman, 1470s,
brush drawing in brown and white on brown linen,
283 x 193 mm.

15

THIS SPLENDID WARRIOR is one of the great drawings of Leonardo's early career. Leonardo manipulated the metalpoint, normally a stiff and unforgiving drawing tool, to create elegant and fluid lines in the fanciful headdress and armour. Details such as the gaping mouth and curling tongue of the lion on the breastplate or the dragon-like wings on the headdress testify to Leonardo's imagination. This type of profile of an ancient warrior was influenced by sculptural reliefs of Alexander the Great and Darius created by Verrocchio and his workshop. It is also equivalent to Verrocchio's beautiful drawings of idealized heads of women, but in this instance Leonardo has not made the warrior's features blandly idealized but has infused the face with character and a fearsome gaze.

Bust of a warrior in profile, c.1475,
metalpoint on cream coloured prepared paper,
285 x 208 mm.

Details of *Bust of a warrior in profile* (p. 17).

SOME TIME IN THE LATE 1470s Leonardo was exploring the possibilities of a composition with a maiden and a unicorn. There are two sketches of the subject on this sheet. The lower one is more difficult to read as it was drawn in leadpoint, but close examination reveals a rapid sketch of a woman caressing the horn of a unicorn. The upper drawing, which is far more legible because it was drawn in pen and ink, is framed by a light outline, suggesting that Leonardo was considering the subject for a painting. Another two drawings in the Ashmolean Museum in Oxford further explore the subject. The image of the mythical unicorn being tamed by a virginal maiden was used as a metaphor for chastity in the Renaissance. It is unclear from these small sketches whether Leonardo intended to create an allegorical painting or a portrait of a young woman with a unicorn (an idea later taken up by Raphael). As was frequently the case, Leonardo never turned these ideas on paper into a finished painting.

Studies of a maiden with a unicorn, late 1470s,
pen and brown ink over leadpoint,
280 x 197 mm.

AROUND THE SAME TIME that Leonardo was exploring a composition with a maiden and a unicorn, he was also making numerous sketches of a mother and child with a cat. The first of the three sheets illustrated here and overleaf is in fact the opposite side of the drawing of the maiden with a unicorn (p. 21), while the other two are recto and verso of a single sheet. Each of these pages is covered with many sketches as Leonardo poured out his ideas on paper. In this respect, these drawings are similar to sheets by Verrocchio, who often used both sides of the paper for a variety of rapidly executed sketches. Leonardo's spirited pen work in each drawing shows his creative thoughts as he attempted to work out how to position the wriggling child and cat in a life-like manner. It appears as if these drawings came directly from Leonardo's imagination rather than from study of live models, but the naturalism of the interaction between child and animal show that observation of the world around him was always behind Leonardo's creations.

Two studies of the Virgin and Child with a cat,
and three studies of the Child with a cat, late 1470s or early 1480s,
pen and brown ink over leadpoint,
280 x 197 mm.

Three studies of the Christ Child with a cat, and one study of a cat,
late 1470s or early 1480s, pen and ink over traces of leadpoint, 212 x 148 mm.

Three studies of the Christ Child with a cat, and one study of a cat,
late 1470s or early 1480s, pen and ink over traces of leadpoint, 212 x 148 mm.

LEONARDO DEVELOPED the idea of a cat desperate to escape from the stifling embrace of an infant into a composition of the Virgin and Child. There are seven surviving drawings for this project, five of which are in the British Museum, but despite these concentrated studies of the composition, no painting seems to have come to fruition. In this drawing, as in the *Maiden with a unicorn* (p. 21), Leonardo created an arched framework to enclose the sketch in the shape of the proposed painting. The child and cat and the upper body of the Virgin are clearly rendered, but the lower body of the Virgin is made up of a tangled mass of furious strokes of the pen. Leonardo was evidently still working out the position of her legs and the folds of her drapery even as he held the pen on the paper. The arched framing and the outline of a window behind the figures is reminiscent of Leonardo's completed painting now called the *Benois Madonna* (Hermitage, St Petersburg), which suggests that these drawings were created during the same period as the painting, probably in the late 1470s or early 1480s before Leonardo left Florence for Milan.

The Virgin and Child with a cat,
late 1470s or early 1480s, pen and ink over stylus, 132 x 96 mm.

To CREATE THIS DRAWING, Leonardo held up the paper to the light and traced the outline of the drawing he had made on the other side to create a mirror image of the Virgin and Child with a cat. The three positions of the Virgin's head and energetic pen lines on the legs show that he was still working out her position, but the pose of the child and the cat are more clearly legible and seem fixed in his mind. The addition of brown ink wash, applied with a brush to pick out the shadows and throw into contrast the areas of brightest light, suggests that Leonardo may have been getting closer to a solution for a composition as he worked out the lighting.

The Virgin and Child with a cat,
late 1470s or early 1480s, pen and ink over stylus, 132 x 96 mm.

A S LEONARDO worked out how he would portray the Christ Child
holding a cat, he must have been keenly aware of cats in his
environment. In this carefully observed metalpoint drawing, he made
two separate studies from different angles of a cat washing itself and a
third drawing of a dog. In his notebooks, Leonardo recommended that
artists should always have a drawing pad handy so as to make quick
sketches of things that they saw. Such naturalistic, informal drawings
were vital means for Leonardo to study and analyse the world around
him.

Two studies of a cat and one of a dog, late 1470s or early 1480s,

metalpoint on cream coloured prepared paper,

139 x 104 mm.

THE COMBINATION of facial profiles, a study of a mother and child and scientific studies all on the same sheet of paper give an insight into the unusual digressions of Leonardo's curious mind. One can imagine that as he continued to work out a composition of the Virgin and Child, his attention was drawn to exploring the mechanical contraption then to the faces as his mind leapt from one idea to another. He began this sheet in leadpoint, a technique similar to modern graphite that created a thin, slightly lustrous line which, unlike metalpoint, did not require any preparation of the surface. He later simplified and reinforced the sketch of the mother and child with pen and ink to clarify his favoured design.

Virgin and Child, profiles and other technical sketches, late 1470s,
leadpoint and pen and ink on pink prepared paper,
200 x 153 mm.

O N THE OTHER SIDE of the sheet of the *Virgin and Child, profiles and other technical sketches* (p. 33), Leonardo made three further studies of a mother and child. As on the verso, he began drawing with quick sketches in leadpoint and then reinforced the drawings in pen and ink. The faint sketch below the two ink drawings was not reinforced in ink and gives a better idea of the rapid nature of the underlying leadpoint drawing. Another sheet in the Uffizi in Florence with similar sketches to the recto and verso of this drawing bears Leonardo's inscription, '1478, I began two Virgin Marys'. It is notoriously difficult to date the majority of Leonardo's works, so this small annotation is key to pinning these studies of the Virgin and Child to the late 1470s. The drawing inscribed by an arch on the right of the sheet is close to the final composition of the *Benois Madonna* which is assumed to be one of the images of the Virgin referred to in Leonardo's note. The lower leadpoint drawing is close to the painting now called the *Madonna Litta* (also in the Hermitage, St Petersburg) that can also be assumed to be of a similar date.

Studies of the Virgin and Child, late 1470s,
pen and ink with leadpoint on unprepared paper,
200 x 153 mm.

THIS STUDY of an angel is a good example of how notoriously difficult it is to date works by Leonardo. Some scholars believe that the dense pen work and complexity of pose of this drawing are similar to the sketches of a child with a cat (pp. 24–5) and thus date it to the early 1480s, while others point to the similarity to the angel on the right in the *Baptism of Christ* by Verrocchio (Uffizi, Florence) painted in or around 1476 and so suggest that it must have been drawn earlier. The handling of the ink, especially the dense hatching in the folds of drapery, and the S-curve of the angel's body are reminiscent of the child and cat, but the pose of the angel, especially the upturned head, is indeed similar to Verrocchio's altarpiece. The angels in the *Baptism* are thought to have been painted by Leonardo while he was in Verrocchio's workshop and are often cited as an example of how the young Leonardo exceeded the talent of his master. The drawing, undoubtedly a fragment of a once-larger sheet, demonstrates Leonardo's characteristic working out of ideas as he drew. The two positions of the upraised arm and the slight sketch of another possible pose below show the progress of his ideas even as he drew the pen across the paper.

A kneeling angel, late 1470s or early 1480s,
pen and ink over leadpoint,
123 x 61 mm.

THIS RELATIVELY SLIGHT SKETCH of a woman carrying a child is a marvellous example of how a great draughtsman can convey so much in so few strokes of the pen. Leonardo drew the figures in outline with little or no attention to contour or shading, and yet details such as the volume of the woman's body and the complex twist of the child's body are immediately apparent. The simple, curved lines that describe the folds of drapery give a sense of how she is dressed, but the confident outlines of her body show that Leonardo conceived the figure as naked with her clothing as an afterthought. Again, the dating of this sheet is much disputed, but its economical line is stylistically similar to works Leonardo made at the end of his first Florentine period in the early 1480s.

A woman carrying a child, early 1480s,
pen and ink over stylus underdrawing,
123 x 87 mm.

I N THE SUMMER OF 1481 the monks of San Donato a Scopeto commissioned Leonardo to paint an altarpiece for their church just outside Florence's city walls. Leonardo's father, a well-connected notary in Florence, undoubtedly secured the commission for his son and then drafted the contract with the monks. The subject of the altarpiece is not recorded but is assumed to be the unfinished *Adoration of the Magi* now in the Uffizi. The many drawings for this project show that Leonardo planned a radically new interpretation of the subject, with the Virgin and Child in front of a dense crowd of figures and battling horsemen. The bulk of the extant drawings for the *Adoration* are, like this one, studies of groups of figures who react in different ways to the sight of the newborn Christ. The two figures at the centre of this sheet, including the draped man with his chin in his hand and the nude leaning on a staff, are studies for a figure on the left of the composition. The other drawings on this sheet do not relate so closely to the painting and so it is unclear if they are unrealized ideas for the *Adoration* or, as was commonly the case with Leonardo, sketches for a different project conceived at the same moment.

40

Study of six figures and a profile, c.1480–81,
pen and ink, 163 x 263 mm.

D ESPITE THE MANY surviving drawings for the *Adoration*, the panel
now in the Uffizi never went beyond a monotone underpainting.
The surviving drawings are therefore very important to help to understand Leonardo's intentions. This sheet with its two pairs of figures, at
the top a man blowing a trumpet into the ear of another and below two
seated men engaged in a lively dispute, has been connected to the
Adoration through other preparatory drawings now in the Louvre and the
Uffizi. The men do not appear in the painting as they do here, but it
seems clear that Leonardo designed them for the background of the
picture where his imagination appears to have run wild in creating a
scene of ruined architecture, auxiliary figures and horsemen.

A man blowing a trumpet into the ear of a nude man, and two seated men,
c. 1480–81, pen and ink over stylus, 258 x 193 mm.

THIS HORSEMAN, without the dragon, appears in the background of the *Adoration of the Magi*, to the right of the trunk of the central tree. Created by only a few strokes of the pen to set down the outlines and then blocked in with a brush charged with ink wash, the drawing is a masterful depiction of the anger of the soldier on horseback and the energy of the battle between him and the fierce dragon. The complex S-curve of the rearing horse's body demonstrates Leonardo's fascination with depicting movement on a two-dimensional surface. Considering the numerous preparatory studies for incidental figures to the *Adoration*, it becomes apparent that the design process held more fascination for Leonardo than the finishing of the painting. Leonardo abandoned the incomplete panel of the *Adoration* when he left Florence for Milan in 1482. Perhaps he lacked the patience to realize in paint the complex composition that he had conceived in his head. Because of Leonardo's departure, the monks at San Donato were left without an altarpiece for over a decade, until Filippino Lippi completed another painting of the same subject to substitute for Leonardo's abandoned work.

*A horseman fighting a dragon, c.*1480–81,
pen and ink with wash, 138 x 190 mm.

THIS COMPLEX ALLEGORY is drawn on the verso of the *Study of six figures and a profile* (p. 41), thereby making it possible to date the sheet to the same time as Leonardo's preliminary work on the San Donato a Scopeto *Adoration*. He drew the complex composition in metalpoint, labelling the figures to identify them. Later, he reinforced the centre and right side of the drawing with ink applied with a pen and a brush. The central group in the drawing depicts the tightly knitted figures of Death with Envy and Ineptitude. Death brandishes a flaming torch, pointing it towards a tree, but the flames are stopped from licking the branches by a putto blowing through a trumpet who is held by Fortune. On the far left of the page, Ignorance hovers over Pride. Interestingly, this third of the drawing was not completed in pen, enabling Leonardo's preliminary metalwork drawing to be fully visible. The intended meaning of the drawing is now obscure, but allegorical depictions of Fortune seem to have interested Leonardo at this phase of his career.

Allegory with Fortune, late 1470s or early 1480s,
metalpoint with pen and ink on pink prepared paper,
163 x 263 mm.

A S IN THE PREVIOUS SHEET, the underlying subject of the allegory depicted in this sheet is now difficult to understand, but Leonardo's remarkable ink brushwork has stood the test of time. He began this drawing with extensive underdrawing with the point of a stylus. These nearly invisible lines enabled him to then use ink with both the nib of a pen and the point of a brush to create seemingly effortless, flowing lines. The personification of Fortune may be identified by her long hair that blows forward over her head. As she hovers in the air, she appears to cover a fire above a tree stump and trophies with another shield. Above the larger drawing of Fortune is an alternative view of her head created in pen and ink while at the top left a second figure, probably a winged personification of Fame, flies out of the darkness.

Study of a winged figure, and allegory with Fortune, c.1482–5,
pen and ink with wash over stylus, independent sketches in stylus,
249 x 202 mm.

LEONARDO presented himself to the Sforza court in Milan with a letter promoting his talents as a military engineer, architect and artist specializing in both sculpture and painting. He appeals to the need for military defences and weapons, stating that he could design superior portable bridges, cannons and catapults as well as clever methods of attacking fortified towns. He writes: 'Also I can make armoured cars, safe and unassailable, which will enter the serried ranks of the enemy with their artillery, and there is no company of men at arms so great that they will break it. And behind these the infantry will be able to follow quite unharmed and without any opposition.' This drawing demonstrates some of Leonardo's inventive if impractical ideas for a beetle-like tank and fearsome revolving scythes powered by soldiers on horseback. He annotated the drawing with helpful comments such as 'when this travels through your men, you will wish to raise the shafts of the scythes so that you will not injure anyone on your side' and, by the tank on the right, 'this is good for breaking the ranks, but you will want to follow it up.'

Sketches of military machinery, mid 1480s, pen and ink, 173 x 245 mm.

THE OUSTING of the Medici family, the creation of the Florentine Republic and the election of Piero Soderini as its new leader ensured that the Florence to which Leonardo returned in 1503 was politically a much different place than the one he had left in the 1480s. Soderini, eager to boost the reputation of his new government, commissioned Leonardo and Michelangelo to paint murals commemorating historical Florentine victories on the walls of the new council chamber. It was a rare moment when both of the greatest living Florentine artists were resident in their native city. The opportunity to pit them against each other must have created a highly charged working environment. Leonardo's subject, the *Battle of Anghiari*, celebrated the Florentine defeat of the Milanese in June 1440. He created numerous preparatory drawings for the painting, many of which include charging horses and angry soldiers engaged in a lively battle. In May 1504 Leonardo was painting the central section of the mural depicting the Florentine fight to win the Milanese standard. He used an experimental oil and fresco technique that proved ill suited to wall painting and, within a short time of its application, the work disintegrated. Nevertheless, Leonardo's life-sized cartoon for the project is well documented and became a focus of pilgrimage for younger artists to study his style.

Studies of horsemen, c.1503–4,
pen and ink, 83 x 120 mm.

THIS RAPIDLY SKETCHED black chalk drawing of a lunging man appears on the verso of the *Studies of horsemen*. Although it is not as easily connected to the *Fight for the Standard* as the recto, it is very likely to be another study for the *Battle of Anghiari*. The rapid style of the chalk and unpolished finish of the drawing suggest that Leonardo made this quick sketch to explore a pose he was working out in his head. Given that the painting no longer survives, even these small, apparently insignificant drawings become vital clues to the make-up of this hugely important commission. The disintegration of the mural on the walls of the council chamber was so acute that only sixty years later in 1563 Giorgio Vasari completely covered over what was left of Leonardo's painting with a new fresco. There has been much speculation about what, if any, of Leonardo's work survives under Vasari's later painting, but considering Vasari's deep reverence for the Florentine artists who preceded him, it seems unlikely that he would have covered up any salvageable work.

*A man lunging, c.*1503–4,
black chalk, 83 x 120 mm.

THE HIGHLY WORKED black chalk figure group at the centre of this sheet represents an early invention for the composition of the Virgin with the infant Christ on her lap flanked by her mother St Anne and the infant St John the Baptist that Leonardo further developed in the large cartoon now in the National Gallery, London (p. 12). The central figure group is framed with a simple outline as in the *Maiden with a unicorn* (p. 21), which in this case is also measured by regular pinpricks along the bottom and left side to set the scale for enlargement to the final scale of the painting. The main figure group is surrounded by further smaller sketches of individual figures or pairs of figures and technical drawings for a hydraulic project. The addition of the technical drawings is characteristic of Leonardo's roving mind. It seems as if he had trouble keeping his thoughts on a single subject as he worked out both a painting and an engineering task at the same time. The dating of this drawing and the National Gallery cartoon has been much disputed, but the general consensus is that they were created some time in the first decade of the sixteenth century.

Studies for the Virgin and Child with St Anne and the infant St John the Baptist, and machinery, c.1500–10, pen and ink, grey wash over black chalk and stylus, 267 x 201 mm.

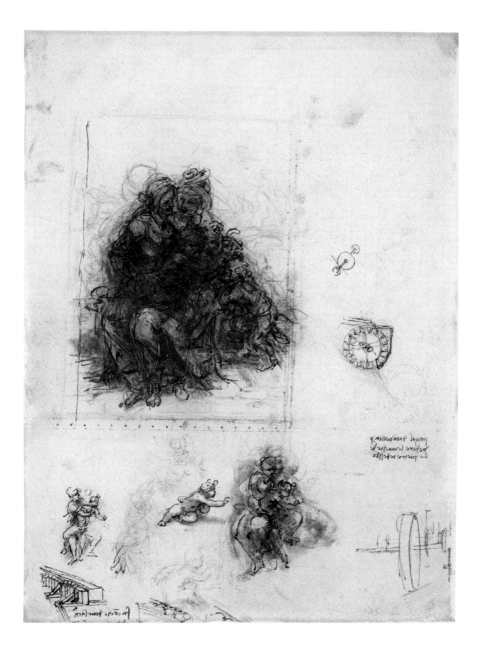

As LEONARDO developed the framed figure group on the recto of this sheet (p. 57), he built up successive layers of chalk, wash applied with a brush and ink applied with a pen to such an extent that details of the group, especially the Christ Child in the lap of the Virgin, are almost impossible to decipher. To aid legibility, Leonardo turned over the paper and made a rough tracing of the figure group on the opposite side. Because this is a tracing, the figures appear in reverse to their positions on the recto of the sheet. This group, albeit in reverse, is closest to the design Leonardo worked up in the large cartoon now in the National Gallery (p. 12). It is known through written sources and surviving paintings and drawings that Leonardo was occupied with at least four versions of this composition. Of these, only the National Gallery cartoon and the painting of *The Virgin and Child with St Anne* in the Louvre survive. The more highly worked-up head of a man that appears upside down in relation to the figure group may have already been on the page when Leonardo traced the design through from the other side. It has not been connected to any particular composition, but it is characteristic of Leonardo's personality-filled faces and remarkably similar to the hook-nosed *Bust of a warrior in profile* (p. 17) from earlier in his career.

Virgin and Child with St Anne and the infant St John the Baptist, and male profile,
*c.*1500–10, black chalk and stylus, 267 x 201 mm.

THE BLACK CHALK PROFILE of a curly-haired man that appears upside down on the previous sheet (p. 59) is similar in physiognomy to this red chalk profile of a bald man. Leonardo's vivid depiction of the folds of the skin, the bald head and the bulbous vein in the cheek testify to his study of dissected corpses. These signs of physical decay contrast with the figure's resolute character conveyed by his jutting chin and bold stare. Red chalk, a broad line medium that could be used to create a range of tone, was one that Leonardo adopted in the 1490s while in Milan. The variety of shading possible with red chalk may be seen in this sheet in the contrast between the widely spaced broad lines of hatching on the back of the head compared to the densely drawn deep shadow in the eye sockets. Red chalk was well suited to the gradual shading of tones used by Leonardo in his paintings to create a soft, smoky palette of colour.

*Male profile, c.*1490,
red chalk, 102 x 74 mm.

61

COMPARED TO many of the drawings in this book, the penmanship of this nude is remarkably neat and legible. The muscular figure and especially the head and hair are drawn in Leonardo's characteristic style although the direction of the shading in the background is unusual for a left-handed draughtsman. It is probable that the more precise nature of the handling of the pen reflects the purpose of the design. This is not a drawing where Leonardo formulated the pose through trial and error, but one where he seems to have had a clear idea of it before putting pen to paper. A faint black chalk underdrawing is just visible beneath the ink, showing that Leonardo sketched the pose before fixing it in ink. The frontal pose of the nude reflects Leonardo's keen interest in anatomy and accurate rendering of muscles and underlying bone structure. During his lifetime he wrote copious notes on the proportions of the body, with detailed calculations on its measurements such as the distance from the elbow to the hand, the relationship of the size of the head to the size of a foot or the length of the torso. These notebooks, posthumously compiled and edited by Leonardo's pupil and artistic heir Lorenzo Melzi, form an important part of our knowledge of Leonardo's genius.

Nude man holding a staff, 1490s,
pen and ink over black chalk,
108 x 54 mm.

This extraordinarily naturalistic profile of the lower half of a muscular man's body epitomizes Leonardo's interest in the proportions and make-up of the human figure. The careful rendering of the musculature, especially in the calf and on the buttocks, is heightened by the choice of red chalk on a salmon pink background that is nearly the same colour as the chalk itself. Red chalk, which is softer than black chalk and therefore can make very subtle gradations of tone, was not widely used for figure studies at this time, but Leonardo's beautiful drawings helped to popularize it as a more common drawing tool. The extensive range in tone possible with red chalk is analogous to Leonardo's use of oil paint with which he could render far more atmospheric and profound hues than with the more old-fashioned medium of tempera. The purpose of this drawing is not known, but a similarity in subject and technique to another sheet in Windsor suggests that they might once have made up a sketchbook of anatomical drawings.

Abdomen and left leg of a nude man standing in profile, c.1506–8, red chalk on salmon pink prepared paper, 252 x 198 mm.

Leonardo's paintings and drawings are filled with individualized, character-filled personalities. He wrote extensively on the human face, noting observations such as: 'It is true that the signs of faces display in part the nature of men, their vices and temperaments.' He seems to have been particularly interested in grotesque facial features, as through their deformities he was able to convey deep insight into the human character. He advocated making notebooks to record distinctive facial features to aid the artist when he returned to his studio, but in regard to the monstrous faces that feature in so many of his drawings, Leonardo wrote, 'Of grotesque faces I need say nothing, because they are kept in mind without difficulty.' A large number of these caricatures survive, most of which are small-scale drawings cut from larger sheets. The grotesques were widely copied and later engraved as prints, further disseminating Leonardo's creations to a wider audience.

*Caricatures of an old woman and an old man, c.*1508–10,
pen and ink, 57 x 42 mm and 57 x 40 mm.

THE HOMECOMING of Leonardo after a twenty-year absence coupled with the prestigious commission to paint in the council chamber of the newly formed Republican government ensured that work on the *Battle of Anghiari* generated considerable curiosity amongst Florentines. Contemporary accounts relate that in 1504 Leonardo was working on a large cartoon for the central scene depicting the *Fight for the Standard* in a special studio created for him in the church of Santa Maria Novella. By the spring of 1505 he was engaged in painting the scene on the walls of the council chamber, but because of the ephemeral nature of his experimental technique little is known of what he actually completed. Copies after his preliminary drawings, the cartoon and the painting before it degenerated have therefore become vital clues to the lost work. This drawing of an enraged horseman on his charging steed appears to be an early copy after Leonardo's designs. The artist is unknown, but comparison to known preliminary drawings for the mural and to more complete copies after the *Fight for the Standard* which omit many details of this horseman suggest that it was drawn by an artist with access to Leonardo's drawings and cartoon. The subtle shading and highlighting of the horse and the pink prepared paper also suggest that this artist was familiar with Leonardo's drawing methods and technique. We are unlikely to discover the artist's identity, and yet his accomplished copy after Leonardo remains an important record of the master's now-lost invention.

Circle of Leonardo da Vinci, *A horse and horseman*, after 1504, pen and brown ink with brown wash heightened with white on pink prepared paper, 270 x 239 mm.

L EONARDO'S WORKS created during his first period in Milan inspired a group of younger Milanese artists to start painting in his style. During the same period, he began to write down notes on the art and technique of painting that, after his death, were compiled by Francesco Melzi and published as a treatise on painting. The degree to which the young followers of Leonardo, dubbed the 'Leonardeschi' by scholars, may have been directly taught by Leonardo is not entirely clear, but drawings such as this beautifully lit head of a woman suggest that some of them at least had a deep understanding of both Leonardo's paintings and his drawing style. This head is based on the Virgin in Leonardo's *Virgin of the Rocks* (National Gallery, London), a painting that was an important touchstone for the Leonardeschi. The style of this drawing fits with a group of paintings and drawings by an artist who created an altarpiece of the *Virgin and Child surrounded by doctors of the church with Ludovico Sforza and his family* (Brera, Milan), painted in the mid 1490s. Although a corpus of works by this painter has been identified, all attempts to give a name to the artist have been unsuccessful, as the paintings and drawings by his hand do not match the style of any named artist in Leonardo's orbit. He is therefore known as the Master of the Pala Sforzesca or Master of the Sforza Altarpiece.

Master of Pala Sforzesca, *Head of a woman*, mid 1490s, metalpoint on grey-green prepared paper, 242 x 160 mm.

A GROUP OF AROUND fifteen paintings and a handful of drawings have been connected to the Master of the Pala Sforzesca. The Christ Child in this drawing bears a close resemblance to the Infant in the eponymous altarpiece, but is even closer to a painting of the *Virgin and Child with St Roch and donors* formerly in the Cora collection. Because the Master of the Pala Sforzesca is unnamed, the span of his life is unknown, but works attributable to his hand date within a thirty-year period from the last decade of the fifteenth century. The style and technique of this drawing exhibit some of the characteristics of the Leonardeschi. It was made in metalpoint on prepared paper, a technique favoured by Leonardo in his early years. The white heightening does not merely heighten the metalpoint drawing but also defines the figures, making them loom out from the dark background. The pose of the Virgin is again similar to the *Virgin of the Rocks* (National Gallery, London), while the blessing Child stretched across her lap is a reflection of the Christ Child in the National Gallery cartoon (p. 12). Given Leonardo's legendary difficulty in completing paintings, works by his Milanese followers such as the Master of the Pala Sforzesca must have been sought after as examples of the great artist's style.

Master of Pala Sforzesca, *Virgin and Child*,
metalpoint with touches of pen and ink, heightened with
white on blue-green prepared paper, 371 x 296 mm.

G iovanni Agostino da Lodi (active *c.*1467-1524/5) was a Lombard artist who spent his early career in the Veneto working in the style of Giovanni Bellini. By 1510 he had returned to Lombardy and was living in Milan. His works from this period reflect vestiges of Bellini's style coupled with knowledge of Leonardo's drawings and his theories on art. It is not known to what extent Giovanni Agostino had direct contact with the Florentine genius. The diffusion of Leonardo's theories on painting inspired his Milanese followers to be keen observers of the human face and Giovanni Agostino's idiosyncratic red chalk drawings of heads are among the most distinctive renderings of faces made by any of the Leonardeschi. His faces are not dependent on a prototype by Leonardo, but his choice of red chalk to create smooth depth of tone in the shading and the keen observation of the eccentricities of expressions and individuals are certainly dependent on Leonardo's style.

Attributed to Giovanni Agostino da Lodi,
A curly-haired man with his eyes shut tight,
red chalk, pricked for transfer, 252 x 181 mm.

WHILE THE previous sheet is arresting for the clenched eyes and grimace on the man's face, this drawing is marked by careful consideration of the sitter's sagging skin on his broad neck, deep-set eyes and distinctive nose and mouth. The head studies by Giovanni Agostino are not technically portraits as they were not intended to represent a particular named person, but they are similar to portraiture in their depiction of the variety of personalities he observed in his world. Red chalk became increasingly prevalent in Leonardo's own drawings in the late 1490s, perhaps because he appreciated the broad tonality that the soft chalk was capable of creating on the page. The variety of line and range of colour possible with red chalk is well demonstrated in Giovanni Agostino's drawing. He used the chalk in broad, widely spaced lines in the hair and neck to rapidly convey these areas which were of little interest to his purpose while in the areas of greatest concentration, especially around the deep-set eyes and furrows of wrinkles from the nose to the mouth, he applied and reapplied the chalk to make deep, dark hues of shade.

Giovanni Agostino da Lodi,
Head of a man in profile,
red chalk, 175 x 130 mm.

Leonardo da Vinci

THE TWO LEONARDESCHI who are most closely associated with Leonardo's Milanese workshop are Marco d'Oggiono (*c*.1467–1524) and Giovanni Antonio Boltraffio (1467–1516), who are documented as painters working under Leonardo in the 1490s. There is evidence that these painters, both aged well into their twenties in the early 1490s, were qualified artists hired by Leonardo to help him complete painting projects in a studio that was also bustling with architectural and sculptural projects. A picture of the inherent jealousies of the various personalities in the workshop emerges in 1491 when both d'Oggiono and Boltraffio were living under Leonardo's roof and accused another assistant called Giacomo Salaì of stealing silverpoint drawings belonging to the pair. This metalpoint study for billowing drapery may have been the type of work that caught Salaì's fancy. It is an accomplished study in light and shade that looms out from the darkened background. It is a study for an altarpiece of the *Resurrection of Christ* (Gemäldegalerie, Berlin) that was a collaboration between d'Oggiono and Boltraffio commissioned in 1491. The drapery study is often attributed to d'Oggiono, but the close working relationship of these two painters in the early 1490s makes it difficult to distinguish one hand from the other.

Attributed to Marco d'Oggiono or Giovanni Antonio Boltraffio, *Drapery study for the Resurrection of Christ*, 1491–4, metalpoint heightened with white on blue prepared paper, 180 x 155 mm.

Andrea Solario (*c.*1465–1524), like Giovanni Agostino da Lodi, was a Milanese artist whose early career was spent in Venice. By 1524 he had returned to the city of his birth and was working as an established artist. Unlike d'Oggiono and Boltraffio, who were employed by Leonardo, Solario seems to have always been independent of Leonardo's orbit. Solario's rise to fame was closely tied to the political fortunes of Milan. In 1499, when King Louis XII of France and his prime minister Cardinal Georges d'Amboise seized power from Ludovico Sforza, new opportunities opened for artists like Solario. Cardinal d'Amboise took Italian architects and craftsmen with him back to France where he was rebuilding his summer residence at Gaillon near Rouen. Around 1507 he called Solario to France to make paintings in the chapel of his château. During the next three years, Solario remained in the Cardinal's employ. This composition drawing was made for Solario's *Lamentation* (now Louvre, Paris), which is emblazoned with the Amboise arms. The painting is even more dependent on Leonardesque prototypes as the kneeling woman on the right of the drawing was replaced with a kneeling St John whose pose is copied from Leonardo's *Virgin of the Rocks*. Solario's sojourn in France predates Leonardo's, making him an important ambassador of the Italian style to French taste.

Andrea Solario, *Lamentation over the dead Christ*, 1507–10, pen and brown ink with some grey ink and grey wash over black chalk underdrawing, 189 x 186 mm.

B ERNARDINO LUINI (*c.* 1482–1532) was one of the most gifted of the Leonardeschi, who not only copied the master but used this knowledge as inspiration to create a new style of his own. No contemporary documents exist to securely connect him to Leonardo's workshop, but later sixteenth-century accounts of Luini describe him as one of Leonardo's pupils. His son Aurelio reputedly owned a notebook of Leonardo's caricatures and the cartoon of the *Virgin and Child with St Anne* (p. 12). Bernardino's own painting of the cartoon (Ambrosiana, Milan) was created with a delicate luminosity that is one of the hallmarks of his style. Similar attention to subtle shading may be seen in the face of this black chalk profile portrait. The darkened background highlights the sitter, making his image loom from the background. He is identified by an old, perhaps original, inscription at the bottom of the page as Biagio Archimboldo, a Milanese painter who is best known as the father of Giuseppe Archimboldo, painter to the Hapsburg court, who created fanciful heads from fruits and vegetables.

Bernardino Luini, *Portrait of Biagio Archimboldo*, black chalk with blue-black wash, 234 x 146 mm.

THE EARLY CAREER of Girolamo Figino (1548–1608) represents the enduring legacy of Leonardo's teachings in Milan nearly a century after his birth. Figino's master, Giovanni Paolo Lomazzo, was a collector of Leonardo's drawings. In keeping with Leonardo's advice to aspiring painters to copy works of the great masters, Figino's training was based on studies after Leonardo's paintings and drawings. This sheet depicting the Virgin and Child with an unidentified bishop adoring the baby Jesus demonstrates the lessons Figino learned from his training with Lomazzo. The use of red chalk on pink prepared paper is the same technique as Leonardo's own red on such red drawings as the *Abdomen and left leg of a nude man standing in profile* (p. 65). The tender glance shared by the Virgin and her child is redolent of Leonardo's Milanese paintings and of the maternal devotion in drawings such as the *Studies of the Virgin and Child* (p. 23). Finally, the rocky landscape in the background of Figino's drawing is similar to the dramatic landscapes seen in the background of many of Leonardo's paintings. Figino's drawing was made in preparation for a picture depicting the *Holy Family with San Siro*, painted for the sacristy of San Marco, Milan, which can be documented to 1569.

Girolamo Figino, *The Virgin and Child with a bishop*, 1569,
red chalk on pink prepared paper, 306 x 184 mm.

S EVERAL DRAWINGS by Leonardo attest to preparations in the first decade of the sixteenth century for a painting of Leda and her children. Leonardo drew two small sketches framed in the manner of the *Maiden with a unicorn* (p. 21) of a kneeling Leda reaching to the right to help her baby emerge from the egg on the verso of a sheet of studies of the *Battle of Anghiari* now in Windsor and two other drawings of a kneeling Leda with the swan and their children on sheets now in Rotterdam and Chatsworth. There is further evidence for a full-size cartoon of Leda, but no additional affirmation of a completed painting by Leonardo's hand. The depiction of Leda with her children is less common than that of Leda caught in a passionate embrace with her lover Jupiter disguised as a swan. As a result of this mortal and divine coupling, Leda gave birth to two eggs containing two sets of twins, Castor and Pollux and Helen and Clytemnestra. This drawing, attributed to the printmaker Giovanni Battista Palumba, appears to be based on motifs created by Leonardo. It is not clear if the entire composition is based on a lost Leonardo or if the artist was inspired by Leonardo's ideas to create his own work.

Giovanni Battista Palumba,

Leda and the Swan with Helen, Clytemnestra, Castor and Pollux,

c.1510, pen and ink, 125 x 151 mm.

THE ATTRIBUTION of the previous drawing to Giovanni Battista Palumba is based on the connection to this print, signed on the lower left with the cartouche containing the initials IB with a pigeon. This printmaker was for years identified as Master IB with a Bird before it was recognized that IB could stand for Giovanni Battista and Palumba is the Italian word for pigeon. Details of Palumba's life are not known, but his most active period seems to have been during the first quarter of the sixteenth century. Evidence of knowledge of Leonardo's art in Palumba's works has led to the suggestion that he may have been born in Lombardy. The drawing and the print form a unique picture of the designs of a printmaker. The drawing is in the reverse sense to the print because the impression of the metal plate on the paper creates a reverse copy of the image drawn on to the plate. The composition shows the domestic bliss of Leda and her two sets of twins cavorting with their swan father. The background of the drawing sets the family in front of a grove of trees. This device is based on prints by Dürer and demonstrates that northern printmakers as well as Leonardo were an influence on Palumba's art. In the print, the trees were replaced by a classical ruin.

Giovanni Battista Palumba,
Leda and the Swan with Helen, Clytemnestra, Castor and Pollux,
*c.*1510, print, 153 x 125 mm.

THE FIRST DECADES of the sixteenth century mark the rise of the art of printmaking in Italy. Agostino Veneziano (*c.*1490–*c.*1540) was a member of the workshop of Marcantonio Raimondi (1470/82–1527/34), a Roman printmaker who became well known for his prints after Raphael's designs. After the 1527 Sack of Rome halted artistic production in the city, Agostino fled to his native Venice where he continued to perfect his craft. He later returned to Rome where he is assumed to have died around 1540, but documentation of the latter years of his life is sporadic. Increasing interest in printmaking in Rome before the Sack coincided with the rising fame of Leonardo's genius. It is therefore not surprising that an artist like Agostino would have turned to Leonardo's creations for inspiration. This print does not appear to be a copy after an original work by Leonardo but rather an adaptation of Leonardo's caricatures into a new composition. The disfigured and ugly faces are similar to drawn copies after Leonardo's works found in an album of drawings now in the Louvre and also to Leonardo's own notebooks of caricatures, now lost, such as the one reputedly owned by Aurelio Luini. Agostino's initials and the date 1516 in the upper right corner of the page securely identify this work.

Agostino Veneziano,
Grotesques, 1516,
print, 159 x 128 mm.

ACH OF THESE next two prints is a unique example of an idealized head in the manner of Leonardo. Previously, Leonardo himself was considered the maker of these prints, but now they are thought to be products of his close associates. A drawing of an idealized head with a crown of oak leaves survives in the Louvre that is either the model for the *Profile bust of a young woman wearing a crown of ivy leaves* (p. 94) or a copy of the Leonardo precedent for the print. The inscription on the print, ACHA LE VI, suggests that this cameo-like image may have been the emblem for the Accademia Leonardo da Vinci, a group of artists in Milan that was perhaps started by Leonardo himself. There is little evidence for this academy, but given Leonardo's theories on teaching the art of painting and the keen interest shown in his works by contemporary Milanese artists, it is possible to imagine a group of Leonardo enthusiasts. Together, these two prints demonstrate that fascination with Leonardo's heads was not confined to the grotesque but also encompassed his pursuit of ideal beauty.

School of Leonardo da Vinci,
Profile bust of a young woman with plaited hair,
print, 106 x 75 mm.

·ACHA· ·ĪE·VĪ·

School of Leonardo da Vinci,

Profile bust of a young woman wearing a crown of ivy leaves, print, 136 x 130 mm.

FURTHER READING

MONOGRAPHS AND GENERAL WORKS

D. A. Brown, *Leonardo da Vinci: Origins of a genius*, New Haven and London, 1998.

K. Clark, *Leonardo da Vinci*, Cambridge, 1959.

M. Kemp, *Leonardo da Vinci: The marvellous works of nature and man*, London, 1981.

M. Kemp, ed., *Leonardo on Painting: An anthology of writings by Leonardo da Vinci with a selection of documents relating to his career as an artist*, New Haven and London, 1989.

P. C. Mariani, *Leonardo da Vinci: The complete paintings*, New York, 2000.

J. P. Richter, ed., *The Literary Works of Leonardo da Vinci*, London, 1970.

F. Zollner and J. Nathan, *Leonardo*, Cologne and London, 2003.

PRINTS AND DRAWINGS

C. Bambach, ed., *Leonardo da Vinci Master Draftsman*, exhibition catalogue, Metropolitan Museum of Art, New York, New Haven and London, 2003.

M. Clayton, *Leonardo da Vinci: One hundred drawings from the collection of Her Majesty the Queen*, exhibition catalogue, The Queen's Gallery, Buckingham Palace, 1997.

M. Clayton, *Leonardo da Vinci: The divine and the grotesque*, exhibition catalogue, Holyroodhouse and Buckingham Palace, London, 2002.

A. E. Popham, *The Drawings of Leonardo da Vinci*, London, 1946.

A. E. Popham and P. Pouncey, *Italian Drawings in the Department of Prints and Drawings in the British Museum: The fourteenth and fifteenth centuries*, 2 vols, London, 1950.

ILLUSTRATION REFERENCES

Photographs © The Trustees of the British Museum, courtesy of the Departments
of Prints and Drawings and of Photography and Imaging, unless otherwise noted

page

2 1869,0410.1042 (detail)

7 1895,0915.478 (detail)

12 National Gallery, London (NG 6337)

15 1895,0915.489

17 1895,0915.474

18 1895,0915.474 (detail)

19 1895,0915.474 (detail)

21 1860,0616.98 verso

23 1860,0616.98 recto

24 1857,0110.1 recto

25 1857,0110.1 verso

27 1856,0621.1 verso

29 1856,0621.1 recto

31 1895,0915.477

33 1860,0616.100 recto

35 1860,0616.100 verso

37 1913,0617.1

39 1913,0617.2

41 1886,0609.42 recto

43 1895,0915.478

45 1952,1011.2

47 1886,0609.42 verso

49 1895,0915.482

51 1860,0616.99

53 1854,0513.17 recto

page

55 1854,0513.17 verso

57 1875,0612.17 recto

59 1875,0612.17 verso

61 1900,0824.106, bequeathed by
    Henry Vaughan

63 1860,0616.97

65 1886,0609.41

67 Pp,1.37 and Pp,1.38, bequeathed by
    Richard Payne Knight

69 1895,0915.479

71 1895,0915.475

73 1861,0810.1

75 1895,0915.481

77 1859,0806.76

79 1895,0915.485

81 1895,0915.771

83 1895,0915.767

85 1950,0520.2, donated by Miss
    Eleanor Child

87 1862,1011.199

89 1853,0709.254

91 1854,0614.393

93 1845,0825.583

94 1850,1109.92

96